I am with you

Céline Mangan O.P.

I am with you

Biblical experiences of God

Michael Glazier, Inc.
Wilmington, Delaware

This American edition is published by Michael Glazier, Inc., 1210A King Street, Wilmington, Delaware 19801 by arrangement with Veritas Publications, Dublin.

Library of Congress Catalog Card Number: 78-50795

International Standard Book Number: 0-89453-090-9

Printed in the United States of America

Contents

Introduction

The Bible has often been called a letter from God to man. I would prefer to think of it as a photograph album where we are given an inkling of what God is like in sudden photo-like flashes of inspiration. Sometimes these are over-exposed so that all we get is a dim vision of light. At other times we get homely family pictures of God.

Like an album, the Bible is something to browse over at leisure and each time we come to it we discover new angles of light on the familiar snapshots.

And so I would like to turn over the pages of the Bible album and pick out the "snaps" of God which have been of most help to me in my search for God, in the hope that others will be led to turn the pages for themselves and there discover riches which I have not as yet even glimpsed.

I would like to thank all those who have helped me in this search, in particular the members of my community who have been more than generous also in helping to put shape into the following pages.

1 Snapshots of God

The Unknown is shown
Only by a bend in the known.
Norman Nicholson

It was through the ordinary things of life that the people of Israel discovered its God. We often think of their prophets as men who saw visions and heard God talking to them. But often it is through something very ordinary that the "vision", or "snap" to use our own image, comes. Take the prophet, Jeremiah, for instance; walking along the road one day he sees an almond tree (called the Watchful Tree in Hebrew), the first flowering shrub of the year, and immediately this prompts him to think of God:

> The word of Yahweh was addressed to me asking, "Jeremiah, what do you see?" "I see a branch of the Watchful Tree," I answered. Then Yahweh said, "Well seen! I too watch over my word to see it fulfilled" (*Jeremiah 1:11–12*).

Or another prophet, Amos, sees a bricklayer standing measuring a wall with a plumb-line and

9

this makes him think of God with a plumb-line in his hand measuring his people's behaviour towards their fellow men and finding them wanting.

Jesus himself was an expert at this type of photography. His stories are full of pictorial illustrations of God at work. We are familiar with the pictures of the Good Shepherd with the lost sheep on his shoulders; the Father of the Prodigal Son with his arms wide open to receive his boy; the Good Samaritan binding up the wounds of the man who had fallen among robbers. But, we are not so familiar with the picture of God bending over the baking board, up to his elbows in flour, or in the guise of a pub owner calling from his shop door to allcomers to hurry in and have a drink! And yet these pictures get across very tellingly the involvement of God with his people and the lengths he will go to bring them to himself.

Our trouble is that we tend to take some of the biblical images of God to the exclusion of others, whereas no one image, or even a few, can give the whole picture. We have to throw our preconceptions and "canned" notions to the four winds. In our catechisms, for instance, we had him all neatly "packaged": he was omnipotent, omnipresent and so on. But what do these mean? Omnipotence, in our terms, means power—all power, but the way it works in God's terms seems to us more like weakness. The kind of strength meant is a creative strength, a letting-be. He allows things gently, almost tantalisingly, even playfully, to be themselves.

Now that we no longer need a "God of the gaps" to fill in for our lack of knowledge of nature, science, human behaviour etc., we are better able to appreciate God's essential relationship to us and to realise that life is a gift from him to be used independently and to the full. Man is in charge of his world and every new discovery can be an insight into this playful aspect of God.

The fact of evolution brings this out in a wonderful way. We can be amazed at the world of the infinitely great, all those millions of stars in outer space, but even more so by the world of the infinitely small: the exquisite colour blend of a cock pheasant, the intricate ritual of a butterfly emerging from its cocoon.

And what is meant by omnipotence? We often tend to think of God's all-watchful eye taking in all we do and entering up against us all that is dubious. At the same time, one of the biggest difficulties we have today is in seeing God at the heart of all reality, involved as much, perhaps even more so, in our washing up the dishes as in our loftiest prayers and highly spiritual talks about him. We have tended to push him off into some remote hinterland of our everyday world instead of seeing his presence all around us.

God is the deepest dimension in everything we do. This does not mean that the world is God and that we are immersed in him through our mere presence in it. This would be Pantheism, and one of the truest insights of the Bible is to see that God is separate from the world, separate but not remote. Because we are rooted in him in our depths he is intimately involved in the whole of our lives.

We should not think, therefore, of God's attributes in too static a way. Those that will best describe him for us will be those that are living, dynamic and even playful. The very hiddenness of God in today's world, where he is variously described as "dead", or in "dry dock", is something to be thankful for, because it has helped us to open up to a deeper understanding of what God really means.

The humanness of God

It is difficult for us to know God in himself. It is only as he reveals himself to us in our lives that we can learn something of him. It has been well said that "the only image of God is man" and it is interesting, that in the Bible where God forbids the Israelites to make any representation of him after the manner of the surrounding nations, he seems to have no objection when they speak of him in human terms which might appear to mock his dignity. We saw how Christ likened him to a pub-keeper; he didn't go beyond comparing him to a burglar either. This need hardly surprise us since many of the saints had a similar capacity to steal people's hearts. St Francis de Sales was once so successful in converting a whole town that an old woman cried out from the crowd as he was leaving: "Oh the great thief! Oh God, look at the great thief!" How much more could the Lord himself be called a thief as he steals our hearts for himself.

Human images and human words are all we have to portray God. We are familiar with the picture of God as an architect building the world according to plan which we get in the first pages of the Bible. Then there is the image of God as a shepherd looking after his sheep (e.g. *Psalm 23*), or as a farmer planting his fruit trees (*Isaiah 5*), a refiner of silver (*Isaiah 48:10*), a butcher producing meat for his people (*Numbers 11:31*), a contractor making a road for them to pass over in the wilderness (*Isaiah 43:19*). The list is endless.

The one I like most in this context is the idea of God as a barber:

> On that day the Lord will shave
> with a blade hired from beyond the river . . .
> the head and hairs of the body,
> and take off the beard too (*Isaiah 7:20*).

The king of Israel in the time of the prophet Isaiah had hired the world power, Assyria, to give his local enemies a close shave. Here the prophet is telling him that it is he himself who will be shaved and that his own God will be the barber. God can be a stern God too, but only to those who are sharp in their dealings with their fellow men.

This brings us to the question of political images of God, of which there are many in the Bible. Obviously he is thought of as king and this was fine for the Israelite to whom kingship was meaningful. Another image would be that of judge which to us has connotations of strictness and legality but for the people of the Bible it was much more a question of liberator. If we study the

Book of Judges in the Bible we see that all the stories in it deal with men who saved their people in times of crisis, and so when thinking of their God as judge they were turning to him as someone who would save them in their needs.

Male and female

Perhaps here is the place to mention too that God was not exclusively pictured in male roles. He is often seen as a father but his people could also think of him as a mother:

> Does a woman forget her baby at the breast,
> or fail to cherish the son of her womb?
> Yet even if these forget,
> I will never forget you (*Isaiah 49:15*).

Christ himself could use the female image for God. Who but he would have thought of comparing God to the fussy woman searching for the lost coin and probably exasperating the rest of the household by refusing to give up until she found it (*Luke 15:8–10*).

The album is open and some of the snaps have spilled out, perhaps rather untidily, over the table. In the following pages I would like to pick out those that have most meaning for us today and, in this way, learn a little more about this God of ours in whom "we live and move and have our being" (*Acts 17:28*, Knox).

2 God as liberator

*What makes the desert beautiful
is that somewhere it hides a well*
Antoine de Saint-Exupéry *The Little Prince*

In this book of Saint-Exupéry there is a beautiful
passage where the Little Prince meets a fox. The
fox asks the Little Prince to tame him so that they
can become friends. He explains that in trying to
tame him, the Little Prince must not come too
close the first day but must just sit there a little
way off, silently watching; the next day he may
come closer, and so on.

This is a perfect illustration of God's dealings
with his people. The whole purpose of "taming"
is to be friends, and God seems to have gone about
making friends very shyly and only by slow stages.
And if we change the Saint-Exupéry image from
a fox to a bird, we will realise that it is no use
trying to tame a bird in summer when he has all
the food he wants. The time to tame a bird is
when the snow is on the ground and he comes to
the window looking for crumbs.

It was in the winter of their slavery in Egypt
that God approached the people of Israel in an
effort to be their friend. It was through the physi-

cal experience of being delivered from slavery that they first had a realisation of what their God was like. This picture of God as liberator was one deeply ingrained in their minds and one that would colour all their insights into him from then on. They looked on him as their saviour long before they considered him as creator, and most of us follow the same pattern in our lives. More often than not, it is out of the needs and troubles of life that we will first come to experience God. The experience of him in creation usually comes later.

He is with us

One man among the Israelites was more alert than others to God's approach. Moses had everything that was needed to make him a popular leader of the people: he was not enslaved as they were; he was skilled in all the wisdom of the Egyptians, yet with an ear attuned to the religious feelings of his people. When he tried to be a liberator on his own initiative, however, he only alienated his people and it took long years of deep pondering and heart-searching in exile before he was ready for the task.

We all know the story of the burning bush: Moses felt within himself the burning conviction of God's presence, a presence of someone who cared for his people and who was now asking him to share the burden of this concern and be the one to lead his people out.

The same Moses, however, who had been so quick to try to right wrongs in the past, now shrinks from the gigantic task before him. The following dialogue between God and himself as given in a teenage magazine highlights Moses's difficulty:

Who am I? I'm just another man.
Who am I? A deserter without friends.
Who am I? I freeze up when I speak.
Yes who am I? Unqualified, untrained.

"But I am with you."

Who am I, to think God calls on me?
Who am I, to follow something that I feel?
Who am I, I feel like such a fool?
Who am I, and how can I be sure?
Who am I, scared and sick with doubt?

"But I am with you."

Are you really, God? For sure?

"Indeed I am. I am."

The young people go on to show what this means for them in their own lives and how there is many a situation of present-day slavery in which they are meant to be leaders.

If we are to take on leadership such as that given to Moses we have to be sure that we are the kind of person Moses was, wholly attentive to the time and action that God wants of us in the here and now. Rosemary Haughton, in her book, *Knife Edge of Experience*, gives some guidelines of the kind of attentiveness that should be ours today:

To give help where it is really needed, not where it is easy; to resist the propaganda of evil, even when it is fashionable evil; to accept a lower standard of living even if it means being peculiar; not to wave the popular flag, even the popular Christian flag, when it is obvious that it has not a cross on it; or simply going on searching and apparently standing still because God is still busy over private preparations of his own.

A people condemned to liberty

Moses had led God's people out, but now his troubles were only beginning! He himself knew what freedom was; it would be a much harder task to get this across to the people. It has been well said that as soon as a people are set free, they hurriedly look around to see what new thing they can enslave themselves to.

This is certainly what happened to the people Moses was trying to lead. Murmuring started almost immediately: the desert was bleak; there was not enough to eat and drink; God had only brought them out in order to kill them off in the desert. There is a graphic summing up of their attitude in the *Book of Numbers 11:4-6*.

Moses must have felt that this experience and the person behind it were really inexpressible but that, somehow, there was a tremendous need to put it all into words. This is what has lifted the Israelites' experience of liberation out of the ordinary run of things. Many other peoples have had the experience of liberation but none of them has tried to give expression, as the Israelites have, to something that underlies all human experience but which rarely comes to the surface.

We are familiar with not being able to express the inexpressible in our personal lives. Take marriage for example. Most of the married life of a couple is spent in the ordinary daily humdrum, but their loving relationship gives meaning to their life together. It is no accident that very often, later on in the Bible, the relationship begun in the desert between God and his people finds expression in terms of married love. This is portrayed in the word which is used for this relationship forged in the desert between God and his people. The word is "covenant" and it has all the connotations of the alliance sealed in marriage between man and woman. Ever afterwards this word summed up for them, in the way a wedding ring is a reminder of their mutual pledge for a married couple, the wonder of what had happened to them and how they should respond to that happening. They had accepted as bridegroom a God with whom it is difficult to live. He would always be ahead of them demanding an ever greater response.

Response involves responsibility

Responding is what the ten commandments are all about. It is not likely that Moses came on these commandments literally "out of the blue". The ethics contained in them were probably an integral part of the Near East philosophy of his time. What was unique was the fact that he combined them in the way he did and showed that if his people wanted to respond to their God's loving initiative

towards them, the only way to do so was by showing their willingness to respond to one another.

The first two commandments are a summons to
freedom—those who have been set free must not
go around enslaving themselves again, or trying to
gain control over God as their neighbours were
doing with their gods. The God of freedom cannot
be reduced to magic or to a slot machine type of
operation. It is always a danger in religious people
to think that God is there for their convenience.

The remainder of the commandments spell out
in no uncertain terms that God is anything but
convenient, since they show that if one is to be
faithful to him, one must have a concern for the
rest of his people. In a tribal society on the move,
just as in our sophisticated Western one, the tendency can be to reject the old. We might never
actually consider euthanasia, but how many of us
in effect practise mental euthanasia by ignoring the
old when they are no longer congenial or useful?
Each of the commandments insists that the kind
of society being built up should be one in which
men would show their response to God by the love
and concern they show for each other.

Of course the Israelites repeatedly forgot this
and the task of their prophets all through their
history was to recall them to this original insight,
as when Amos spoke to the people about oppressing
the poor to gain wealth for themselves:

> Woe to those ensconced so snugly in Zion
> and to those who feel so safe on the mountain
>   of Samaria . . .

they dine on lambs from the flock . . .
they drink wine by the bowlful,
and use the finest oil for anointing
    themselves. . . .

By lowering the bushel, raising the shekel,
by swindling and tampering with the scales,
we can buy up the poor for money,
and the needy for a pair of sandals
(*Amos 6:1, 4–6; 8:5*).

As the years and centuries went by, therefore, there came a deepening in the people's understanding of the covenant between themselves and God. They saw that it was no longer to be written on stone but in men's hearts (cf. *Jeremiah 31:31*). This was to bring about a new deliverance from slavery, not now from the physical slavery of Egypt but from the slavery of sin. Ultimately it would be in Christ that this possibility would be fully realised.

Liberation and violence

There is one problem very much to the fore at present in the whole area of liberation and it is the question of the necessity of violence to achieve liberation. It is a very real problem for Christians in many parts of the world where institutionalised violence seems incapable of dislodgement and where craft and corruption exist to an appalling degree.

There can be no doubt about it that God is active in our world wherever there is a situation similar to that of the Israelites in Egypt, but I

think it would be true to say also that he will
not always be where we would expect him to be.
He was not with Moses when he took the law
into his own hands and killed the Egyptian. It
was only after a complete change of heart that
Moses led the true liberation. Every act of violence
and every revolution brings a possible escalation
of violence unless accompanied by genuine forgiveness.

Christ nowadays is often likened to a revolutionary and he was a revolutionary, not a perpetrator
of violence but rather its victim. This seems to be
the road for every genuine Christian: trying to
change an unjust society in the light of his Christian principles, but sharing the lot of the one who
died as a revolutionary at the hands of the Romans,
and as a blasphemer at the hands of his fellow
Jews.

> Non-violence is the greatest force at the dis-
> posal of mankind. It is mightier than the
> mightiest weapon of destruction devised by the
> ingenuity of man. Destruction is not the law
> of the humans. Man lives freely by his readiness
> to die, if need be, at the hands of his brother,
> never by killing him.
> *All Men are Brothers: Life and Thoughts of
> Mahatma Gandhi*

Suggested Scripture reading

*Old Testament: Exodus 1–20; 24. New Testament:
The gospel of Mark.*

3 God as creator

*'Twas Paradise on earth a while
and then no more.*
James Clarence Mangan

A friend of mine once asked fifteen people if they believed in Adam and Eve; ten answered straight out that they did not; the other five said they had never thought about it. And yet, if we omit the story of Adam and Eve in the Garden, we miss out on one of the deepest biblical insights into God. Granted, we no longer have to think of it in simplistic terms as an historical happening right at the beginning of our planet. What we have in *Genesis* is a story written to tell a truth about man's human situation rather than an account giving exact biological or scientific details of how life began.

We are well aware now that the Bible has many different kinds of literature: historical writing, poetry, fiction, parables and so on. Each type of writing will have a message to convey but one cannot expect poetry, for example, to put across the message in the same way as an historical presentation. There is a lyrical description in *Psalm 114* of the mountains "skipping like rams and the hills like yearling sheep". This is poetic licence, not historical fact.

The early chapters of the Bible intend, as the Holy See has put it, "to relate in simple and figurative language adapted to the understanding of a less developed people, the fundamental truths underlying the divine plan of salvation, as well as the popular descriptions of the origins of the human race and the chosen people" (Pontifical Biblical Commission, 1948).

What we have, therefore, in these first chapters of *Genesis* is a poetic account of our origins. They tell us some things about the world and about men and women in it and about God, which we would not know if we confined ourselves merely to scientific accounts of the beginning of the world. Science answers the question "how", not the question "why". Our problem about the question "why' is that we try to answer it in the same way as the "how". Why is man the way he is? He has tremendous capacities but is somehow flawed, especially in his relationships with others. In our own world, for instance, we have a great dream of progress, yet all around us are wars, hunger, evil. Man suffers from a sense of frustration and is often at cross purposes with his world Why is this so?

The story of Adam and Eve is meant to explain the *why* of all this, rather than the *how*. The writers who composed it were not interested in how man came to be, but in *why* he came to be and in his resulting condition in the world. And so, it has more to tell us about ourselves in the here and now than about our ancestors in the remote past.

Two accounts

If we look at the text of the Bible itself, we will find that there are really two accounts of the beginnings given to us. The first (*Genesis 1—2:4a*) was in fact one of the latest pieces in the Bible to be written down. It is a beautiful hymn of praise to God as creator, with the message coming through clearly: "And God saw all he had made and indeed it was very good." It is the joyful realisation that creation and all that is in it is basically good rather than evil. It is also a clear statement of belief in one God and shows that all the things men worship as gods such as trees, stars and animals are made by God and put under man's control.

This account does not speak of Adam and Eve at all but of mankind:

> God created man in the image of himself,
> in the image of God he created him,
> male and female he created them
> (*Genesis 1:27*).

The author is clearly amazed at the loving care and interest of God in creation and his account shows all the wonder and joy of Israel's new discovery of the closeness of God to the whole of creation.

The second account (*Genesis 2:4b—3:24*) is older than the first and is much more of a story. It is the account we all remember best from our childhood, with its graphic details of the luscious garden, the snake and the apple. This is where we get that homely picture of God, walking in the garden in the cool of the evening, which is meant to give us a vivid idea of God's intimacy with man. We are not meant to take it literally, just as we are not meant to take literally that man was formed out of clay—this is a poetic way of showing man's closeness to earth—or that woman was made from Adam's rib, which is meant to show woman's closeness to man. What we have in the story of the garden, therefore, is an evocation of the harmony and concord that should exist between God, man, woman and the world. God has called man to share his own life; if man refuses this he will upset the balance of everything else.

Man lowers his sights

The picture of harmony which was symbolised by the garden portrays man as he could be; but the story goes on to show man taking a short cut to power. I sometimes wonder if taking short cuts is not man's besetting sin. We destroy the balance of nature by the short cut of deforestation and so cause deep climatic trouble. We take short cuts in human relationships and destroy slowly evolving friendships.

The taking of a short cut is surely what is involved in the story of the Fall. Instead of opting for God, the first human beings "lowered their sights, sought in some way to evade the challenge and transmitted to the generations that followed them, not the pure tradition of fidelity to God's call in all their lives but rather a tradition in which sin or the estrangement from God played a dominant part" (Mackey *Life and Grace*). The terrible thing about sin is that its harmful effects always fall back on man. When the harmony of the relationship with God is destroyed, so is the balance of one's relationship with the world and with one another.

This is what happens with the relations between man and woman. There is no greater charter for woman's rights than those first three chapters of *Genesis* where the absolute equality of man and woman is stressed in contrast to the common practice of the Near East of the time—and indeed practice which has not changed much down to our own times in some areas. The imbalance between man and woman came *after* the Fall (*Genesis 3:16*) and, just as we should be working our way back to the harmony between man and his world, so we should be working for the restoration of the harmony between man and woman also.

The great absence

Lack of harmony, therefore, is a good way of describing what we have traditionally called "original sin". Sin is not a presence of something, it is not a kind of stain on the soul, which only grace can remove. It is much more a question of an absence from God. The accounts of creation, as we saw, tell us that originally man comes from God. Sin is, then, mankind's turning its back on God. Therefore it is a question of the absence of a relationship which should be there. If men and women are absent from God in this way, they cannot pass on to their children their relationship with him, as we saw in the quotation from Mackey's *Life and Grace*. This is what is meant by the transmission of original sin: one cannot pass on what one has not got. There is a story told of Karl Marx's daughter: she had never known God because he was strictly an absence in her upbringing, but when she first heard the *Our Father,* she found herself saying that she could believe in such a God.

Rejection of the Father

How many of us are fully at home with the father image of God? Like the psychoanalyst, Freud, many people, perhaps suffering from a childhood experience of a repressive father, look on God as a powerful authority figure, the decider of good and evil. Perhaps we would like to think of him as a benevolent father striving for the good of his children, and yet we mistrust this image and turn it into that of a tyrant. We see the statement: "Of the tree of the knowledge of good and evil you are not to eat, for on the day you eat of it you shall most surely die", not as the concern of a loving father but as the command of a tyrant, jealous for his privileges.

There is an interesting psychological development in the story of Eve's flirtation with the serpent: at the beginning she stands up for God and even goes too far in his defence, making it seem as if he had forbidden them even to touch the tree: "But of the fruit of the tree in the middle of the garden God said, 'You must not eat it, nor touch it, under pain of death.'" In her defence, she has already twisted the statement around from that of the concerned God to the tyrant, and it is an easy step from there to the final outcome of the temptation.

Our experience of sin gives us a warped outlook on life and on God. Christ's picture of the father in the story of the Prodigal Son is the picture of a loving father with arms thrown wide, ready to forgive and forget. But it is only Christ, the sinless one, who could have drawn such a picture of God. We have "lowered our sights" and only see God in our own image. What would we do to someone who had sinned against us? We would tend to feel like paying him back in the most humiliating way possible, and this is how the son in the story expected to be treated: "Father, I have sinned against heaven and against you; I no longer deserve to be called your son; treat me as one of your paid servants." Actually he would probably have preferred to be on this level of relationship with the father rather than meet the forgiving look of the one he had wronged.

We expect a God who condemns and this colours our whole attitude to law: we see it as coming from a tyrant instead of a liberation making us free to respond as we saw it should do when speaking of the ten commandments in the last chapter. The Jewish religion had at its deepest level this truer insight into the law: the Bible was called the Law, the Torah, and was seen as the gift of

God to his children. Thus, some of the Psalms can speak of the Law as "new life for the soul" (*Psalm 19:7*) and see it as "expanding the heart" (*Psalm 119:32*).

Another garden

It was Christ's own attitude to the Father which opened up for us again the kind of God proposed to us in the story of the garden of Eden and it is interesting that it is in the context of another garden that we see the reversal of what happened in that earlier one. Here, too, there is a temptation: "Father, if you are willing, take this cup away from me . . .", but there is no blurring of the reality of the situation as we saw with Eve. It stands out stark and clear in all its nakedness and horror. Neither does the Father take back the challenge. The purpose of the angel's coming was to comfort Christ, but this does not signify a change in the Father's will. The angel's function was as a trainer to an athlete to prepare him for the contest ahead.

It is in Christ's total commitment to the Father that the reversal of original sin takes place: "As by one man's disobedience many were made sinners, so by one man's obedience many will be made righteous" (*Romans 5:19*). The whole meaning of Christ's atonement is spelt out here: the word literally is *at-one-ment*; the split in our personalities caused by sin is healed. We are made one again with the Father, we learn to know the kind of God we are dealing with. But we will never fully understand this, unless we can say with Christ in the darkest moments of our lives: "Father, let your will be done, not mine."

Suggested Scripture reading

Old Testament: Genesis 1—3. New Testament: Luke 22:39–46.

4 Can God be localised?

> We shall not cease from exploration
> And the end of all our exploring
> Will be to arrive where we started
> And know the place for the first time
>
> T. S. Eliot *Little Gidding*

Our snapshots so far have revealed God coming to
meet man *where he is*: in slavery in Egypt, in sin
in the garden; it is always in man's actual situation
that God will find him. If we were without sin we
would meet God gladly and there would be freedom of speech between us but, as things are, our
first reaction to the overtures of God is to run away
and hide (*Genesis 3:8*), or to forget him in the
bustle of our daily lives. Therefore God has to
pursue us, call to us again and again and try to
catch us off guard, as it were, in order to get a
hearing.

The stories of the Patriarchs give us many a
glimpse into such meetings. There is the description of God surreptitiously revealing himself to
Jacob as he slept (*Genesis 28:10* ff), or their even
more unusual détente during a wrestling match
(*Genesis 32:26–32*). Joseph, sold by his brothers
into slavery, experiences God in an Egyptian prison
(*Genesis 39:21–23*) and we have seen something

already of God's rendezvous with Moses at the burning bush and on Sinai. We must be on the alert to pass beyond our present insight into God and be open to even the most unusual possibilities of meeting him.

Every revelation of himself by God involves an incarnation of himself in human words and images which are influenced by the time and culture, by the physical and even political set-up of those whom he wishes to meet. When the people of Israel settled down in the Promised Land, therefore, whole new possibilities of relationships with him were opened up for them. It was through their leaders very often that each new insight was brought home to them.

Leadership among the people had always been exercised by gifted individuals who had come to the fore in times of crisis. Some were great military leaders such as Joshua, Gideon and Samson, who rescued their people from the hands of their enemies. Others were spiritual leaders, who passed on their own true insight into God and so helped to deepen their people's experience of him. Such a man was Samuel. Most people will be familiar with the appealing story of his call:

> Yahweh called, "Samuel! Samuel!" He answered, "Here I am." Then he ran to Eli and said, "Here I am, since you called me." Eli said, "I did not call. Go back and lie down." So he went and lay down. Once again Yahweh called, "Samuel! Samuel!" Samuel got up and went to Eli and said, "Here I am, since you called me." He replied, "I did not call you, my son;

go back and lie down." Samuel had as yet no knowledge of Yahweh and the word of Yahweh had not yet been revealed to him. Once again Yahweh called, the third time. He got up and went to Eli and said, "Here I am, since you called me." Eli then understood that it was Yahweh who was calling the boy, and he said to Samuel, "Go and lie down, and if someone calls say, 'Speak, Yahweh, your servant is listening.'" So Samuel went and lay in his place. Yahweh then came and stood by, calling as he had done before, "Samuel! Samuel!" Samuel answered, "Speak, Yahweh, your servant is listening" (*I Samuel 3:1–11*).

This is a classic description of God's call to man but it is seldom that we are alert enough even to hear, or patient enough to wait, or ready enough to give the final response.

A king like the nations

In his old age, Samuel had to face the people's dissatisfaction with his leadership: they wanted to be like the nations round about them and, by having a king like theirs, have the security of a constant leader and the focus of centralised government, rather than depend haphazardly on the emergence of a gifted individual who would interpret God's dealings with them at any given time. This is always a temptation for us: we like to have our securities lined up for us in advance instead of trusting a loving Father. Ever afterwards in the history of the people there were those who insisted that kingship was a betrayal of their original insight into God in the desert. But, on the other hand, there were also those who claimed that God had come to meet them in a new way through the monarchy, and certainly their early experiences of kingship seemed to bear this out. There was David, after all, a man who, with all his faults and sins was always ready to return to God and meet him face to face in repentance.

David's story is like a cine-film of man's reactions to the God who comes to meet him: there is his loyalty to God in the midst of Saul's persecution; there is his joyous celebration of his friendship with God in song and dance. One recalls, for example, the picture of his leaping and dancing for joy before the Ark of the Lord on its way to the new city, Jerusalem, which he had specially prepared to receive it (2 *Samuel 6:14–23*). Michal, his wife, sneered at him for acting in a way unbecoming to his dignity as king. David's reply to her is perfectly straightforward:

> I was dancing for Yahweh not for the serving girls. As Yahweh lives, who chose me in preference to your father and his whole House to make me leader of Israel, Yahweh's people, I shall dance before Yahweh and demean myself even more. In your eyes I may be base, but by the maids you speak of I shall be held in honour.

It is the answer of a man who lives from the heart, as David did, to one who put human prestige and self-respect before the service of God. Interestingly enough, an image often used for God nowadays is that of "Lord of the Dance". God, like an expert partner in a dance, can adjust himself to all our false steps and lead us gradually into perfect rhythm with himself.

David certainly took a long time to learn this perfect rhythm and right to the day of his death he was not able to bring it about in his own household. One of his sons even rose in rebellion against him, and we are treated to the sad spectacle of David in his old age in flight before the army of his son. The most moving part of this story comes at the end when the son is finally defeated in battle: one of the soldiers reports to the king that his son has been killed. He expected that he would be full of joy at the news; instead David broke down and burst into tears: " 'My son Absalom! My son! My son Absalom!', he said, 'Would I had died in your place' " (2 *Samuel* 19:1). In his anguish over the death of the son who had wronged him, David is a perfect picture of the God who loved his children so much that he was prepared to give his life for them. Is not this, after all, what the death of Christ reveals to us?

David had kept the basic orientation of his people towards God, but when his son, Solomon, came to the throne, things took a turn for the worse. His reign, at least in its early years, was the nearest Israel ever came to being a world power but his commercial and diplomatic successes were achieved at the cost of the quality of the life of his people. Samuel had long ago told them what they would suffer from a king but they had not listened and now were only too much aware of the truth of his predictions:

These will be the rights of the king who is to reign over you. He will take your sons and assign them to his chariotry and cavalry.... He will also take your daughters as perfumers, cooks and bakers. He will take the best of your fields, of your vineyards and olive groves and give them to his officials... (*1 Samuel 8:11-14*).

In our times we have become very much aware of the damage this kind of hyper-bureaucracy can do to a people; the writings of Alexander Solzhenitsyn, for example, show its results on a whole generation of the Russian people.

Tying God down

I suppose it can be said that Solomon's greatest achievement was the building of the temple in Jerusalem. This city had been made the capital by David but it was only in Solomon's time that the temple was actually built. Up to this, God's presence with his people had often been seen as something very personal. Certainly he could be experienced in a special place, as we have seen already with Moses and Jacob, and the tendency ever afterwards was to make that special place a place of meeting where one could later meet God by appointment, as it were. During their wanderings in the desert, the location of his presence was not in a particular spot but in the people themselves, and the Ark and the pillar of fire that went with them only symbolised that presence. But with the settlement in the land and the setting up of the capital city, Jerusalem, there was a growing tendency to make God "settle down" too, to pin him down to a place of worship where one could meet him always and not be disturbed by his tendency to crop up in the most unlikely of places.

There was a great deal of value in this localisation of God in David's city, the city that would become for centuries the sign of God's presence with his people. It was right that when they settled down they should have a shrine of his presence in their midst. The localised shrine would remind them that they themselves were the visible sign of his presence in the world. It is in this sense that the temple was a glorious beacon for the true faith of Israelites down the ages as they made their journeys to the sanctuary, year after year, their hearts filled with a joy such as that expressed in the following psalm:

> How I rejoiced when they said to me,
> "Let us go to the house of Yahweh!"
> And now our feet are standing
> in your gateways, Jerusalem.
> Jerusalem restored! The city,
> one united whole!
> Here the tribes come up,
> the tribes of Yahweh.
> They come to praise Yahweh's name,
> as he ordered Israel . . . (*Psalm 122*).

This was the true understanding of the place of the temple in Israel's relationship with God but, like all noble ideas, there was nothing easier than to distort this ideal so as to make it seem that the temple gave them a right over God and put them in a privileged position over other nations.

Was it not rather a call to live up to the responsibilities which its presence in their midst demanded of them?

Their mistake was to think that God's promises were unconditional; that just because they had God in their midst they were automatically safe for evermore. It came to the stage that the Israelites, at one period in their history, were saying: "We're all right, our city won't be destroyed; haven't we God's temple (and, therefore, God) safely in our midst?"

It was against such an attitude that the prophet Jeremiah uttered perhaps the most damning denunciations in the Bible:

> Yahweh Sabaoth, the God of Israel, says this: "Amend your behaviour and your actions and I will stay with you here in this place .... Yet steal, would you, murder, commit adultery, perjure yourselves, burn incense to Baal, follow alien gods that you do not know? And then come presenting yourselves in this temple that bears my name, saying: Now we are safe, safe to go on committing all these abominations! Do you take this temple that bears my name for a robbers' den? I, at any rate, am not blind—it is Yahweh who speaks" (*Jeremiah 7:3-11*).

This tendency to confine the divine to a holy place is a characteristic of all ancient religions. We have only to think of our own holy wells, which were pagan shrines before "baptised" by the followers of St Patrick. Of course special places for worship are necessary for us and, as we have seen with the people of Israel, if properly understood, there is no substitute for a place where we can come to meet the one whom we have previously experienced. We are helped by "atmosphere," by symbols and signs of God's presence. We are helped above all by coming together with other members of God's family to celebrate, in great thankfulness, our awareness of God's presence and our need to be reminded of the demands of that presence in our daily lives.

On the other hand, there is a great danger in tying God down to a special place of meeting. This can conveniently keep him at arm's length and degrade the revelation of his presence into a magical presence in mere things and places. And so we can solemnly worship God on Sundays in beautiful Gothic cathedrals, or centemporary new churches, or a place of "pop" liturgy and confine him there for the rest of the week while we get on with the business of living in the crowded bustle of the shopping centre.

We do this in more subtle ways also: we confine God's intervention in life to special places like Lourdes, or to special people like Padre Pio. We never think that perhaps it is our faith and our hands God wishes to use in healing Mrs. Murphy next door, or our lips through which he wishes to give consolation to someone in despair.

We can "localise" God, therefore, and set him up "in state" in our parish churches, as the Israelites did long ago in the temple. But, unless we meet him personally and bring him with us through our cities, towns and countryside, it is a caricature of God that we have set up and not the living God who, in Christ, is nearer to us than we are to ourselves.

Suggested Scripture reading

Old Testament: 1 and 2 Samuel; 1 Kings 1—11; Jeremiah 7. New Testament: Luke 19:28—20:19.

5   The absence of God

*The God who forsakes us
is the God who is with us*
Bonhoeffer *Letters from Prison*

The picture of God quietly domesticated in the Jerusalem temple, there for his people's convenience and politely told not to interfere unduly in their lives, seems a caricature of him rather than a snapshot. It is a caricature, however, that might have many home-truths to tell us, as we have seen. But the usual result of tying God down is that he "breaks out" and becomes a wild disturber of the peace! Or, looking at it from another point of view, one can say that to compel Israel to take a long hard look at its religious practices and beliefs something must happen which would turn these practices and beliefs upside down and inside out.

This was precisely what happened in the capture of their beloved city by the Babylonians in 587 BC: the destruction of the temple and the sending into exile of many of the people. One can sympathise with the Israelites; they were the very race who had given themselves over to God to be his own special people, called by him to make him known in all the world. They saw in him their only refuge from distress, sickness and trouble and

42

yet he seemed now to have withdrawn from them, and left them alone to be plundered by their enemies.

This was the lesson Israel found hardest to learn and the one which hits most of us at one time or another in life: the God we think we know is not God as he really is, and we come to realise that he has to withdraw and hide from us in order that we may come to a truer understanding of him. From this point of view, the whole history of Israel was one continual retreat on God's part, almost like a game of hide-and-seek. When we are in the darkness of despair and trouble we think it very unfair of God to play games and tricks on us. It is only when we come into the light again that we realise he has been leading us all along through strange paths and underground tunnels to a new and much more profound vision of reality.

For the Israelites one result of localising God was that once the temple was destroyed and the people had left their own country for exile, they thought they could no longer worship God at all. This is always a danger in religious practices and beliefs: that God is tied to the way things were always done or, worse still, to one people's particular nationalistic outlook on life. We are more familiar with this attitude here in Ireland than most, but we are not alone in pinning God down in this way. It is always a temptation to think our particular community, be it national or local, has the whole truth about God and religion.

A striking example of this is to be seen in a play by Fritz Hochwaelder: *The Strong are Lonely.*

It is the story of the Jesuit settlement in Paraguay in the eighteenth century, set up as a near-Utopian state to protect the local Indian people from the slave-dealing Spanish colonials. They were a "judgment" community for their fellow Spaniards, as they tried to apply basic Christian principles to everyday living. But it was only when they realised that the Indians were willing to fight on the side of the Jesuit Christ against the "Christ" of the settlers that the superior of the group realised that they themselves were also in need of judgment. They had identified the Kingdom of God too closely with Utopia, a Utopia which seemed to exclude the salvation of their enemies.

"Turn and turn again"

What the Israelites needed, also, was a total re-think on their approach to God and they were fortunate in having in their midst men who were capable of doing this, even if they were not always thanked for it. Prophets are troublesome in any society because they generally tell people what they would rather not hear. So the sensitive and retiring Jeremiah learned when he was called to be a prophet to his people:

> I am a daily laughing-stock,
> everybody's butt.
> Each time I speak the word, I have to howl
> and proclaim: "Violence and ruin!"
> The word of Yahweh has meant for me
> insult, derision, all day long (*Jeremiah 20:7–8*).

Jeremiah was called on to warn the people of

the impending doom of their city and to point out that it was the people's own moral backsliding and false security which made the downfall of the city inevitable.

But once the lesson had been learnt the way was wide open for perhaps the deepest insights into God which can be found within the pages of the Bible. We do not know the name of the prophet who drew these insights together; the fruits of his work are to be found in the second part of the *Book of Isaiah* (Chapter 40–55). Because of this the prophet is often called "Deutero-Isaiah" (deutero meaning second), a rather prosaic title for the man who wrote some of the most inspiring poetry of the Bible.

These sixteen chapters of the Bible are almost unique in the whole history of religion. They come from a people who, though broken by defeat and exile, thrill with an exultant joy in the discovery of their God. It is as if they had realised who God was for the first time and words could hardly keep up with all they wanted to say about their discovery. If we are looking for snapshots, we will find them here in plenty: God as father, as mother, as husband, as builder, as craftsman—and many more.

It was when they were in exile in a foreign country that the people came to the full realisation that their God was the one God of all the world and that nothing else that was called a god was real. There is a passage bristling with satire against those who think that the idols men set up as gods are really gods:

The wood carver takes his measurements, out-
lines the image with chalk, carves it with
chisels, following the outline with dividers. He
shapes it to human proportions and gives it a
human face, for it to live in a temple. He cut
down a cedar, or else took a cypress or an oak
which he selected from the trees in the
forest. . . . For the common man it is so much
fuel; he uses it to warm himself, he also burns
it to bake his bread. But this fellow makes a
god of it and worships it; he makes an idol of
it and bows down before it. . . . "Save me," he
says "because you are my god"
(*Isaiah 44:13-17*).

Perhaps we are not as far as we might hope from
such obvious worship of idols, when there are those
among us who spend their Sunday morning bow-
ing and scraping before their latest Audi!

Console my people

The most revealing picture of God in this part
of the Bible is the renewal of the saviour image,
as the Israelites look to him to lead them in a
second Exodus from their new place of slavery.
But this time it will no longer be a leader from
among their own people who will point the way.
The instrument of salvation will now be someone
who does not even believe in God, namely Cyrus
the Persian who had overthrown the Babylonian
kingdom which was the cause of Israel's downfall
in the first place. It was Cyrus's policy to resettle
in their own land those peoples who had been up-
rooted by his predecessors and even to give
financial and other aid to bring this about.

The insight of the prophet here is a big step forward in Israel's understanding of God's action in the world. It is one which we are still only learning: God does not necessarily intervene directly in his people's lives. The events of history can work together for the furthering of man's journey towards God. Very often, it will be a Cyrus who will be instrumental in forwarding our knowledge of God.

God in dry dock

This is the title of a chapter in a book by one of the best known theologians in the Church today (Schillebeeckx *God and Man*). He is talking about the experience of many of our contemporaries who feel that God is, for all practical purposes, absent from our world. When we try to get a photograph of him, all we register is a blank or at the most a dim negative. But just as the negative is necessary to even the most brilliant film, so the experience of the "absence of God" can be a real help to our coming to know God, the real God, at a very much deeper level.

We live in a world of instant coffee, instant soup, instant everything. It is a world constantly on the move. But the kind of language many of us heard about God as we grew up tended to be static, looking to the past. Many people in our world just ignore rather than deliberately reject such a God. To them he is definitely "high and dry", safely confined to the dead tomes of outmoded theology books or to the draughty churches which they no longer frequent. They "usher God to the edge of his universe and bow him out with thanks for past services rendered".

It has taken us some time to realise that what was happening here was much more a question of a change of culture than a change in religion; that, in the last fifty years or so, we had moved from a largely settled, rural type of culture, with its roots firmly and solidly fixed in the past, to a much more dynamic, quick-moving, alert, urbanised culture which looks towards the future. As the Vatican document, *The Church in the Modern World,* puts it: "We are passing from a relatively static outlook to a more dynamic and evolutionary conception of things. This gives rise to many new problems which demand an entirely fresh approach" (paragraph 5, Grail translation).

The images we use for God will always be taken from the culture in which we find ourselves and so, naturally, in the static culture which was present in Ireland until very recently, we had a static picture of God. Now many of those who are alive to the new culture in which we live are doing just what the Vatican Council suggested and are coming up with "an entirely fresh approach". This may be disconcerting for those of us who have been brought up in the old way. There is nothing against our looking to whatever images we are used to, since they all have some value, but we must allow those who are brought up in a completely different culture pattern from ours to think and speak in ways that mean something to them. Otherwise a whole generation and more may lose God altogether. As Pope Paul has said in his Encyclical on Justice and Peace, 1971: "The Church travels forward with humanity and shares its lot in the setting of history."

"Behold I will make all things new"

An interesting thing is that the newer, more dynamic way of speaking of God, of seeing him as the one who is ahead of us, "renewing the face of the earth", is in many ways far nearer to the biblical conception of God. We have seen something of this already in God's revelation of himself to Moses as the one who would lead his people out and be their liberator, and in his breaking through their efforts to confine him in the temple.

It was really the Israelites who discovered, through their own, often bitter, experiences, this forward-looking thrust towards the future for humanity. Other ancient peoples did not have it. We, as Christians, inherited this historical approach from them. When the early Church, however, came into contact with the Greek way of thinking, it took over more static modes of thought, but Christianity for several hundred years never lost sight of the movement towards the future, towards the final "in-breaking" of God into his world. It was only in the last few hundred years, and for reasons which had largely nothing to do with religion, that we tied God down again and reverted to a narrow religious outlook.

As we have seen, when this happens, God's tendency is to explode! And this explosion is what we are experiencing now in the Church. Even if there are many unusual and bizarre ideas abroad, the Spirit of God certainly seems to have come into his own in the Church again. St John tells us that we should "test the spirits" (*1 John 4:1*). At the same time we are told not to "suppress the Spirit" (*1 Thessalonians 5:19*). And so we can welcome this wonderful "fresh approach" to God and feel liberated to think of him, not as old and battered and broken down, "in dry dock", but as gloriously alive and life-giving, taking us forward with him so that we, too, will "have strength to grasp the breadth and the length, the height and the depth; until, knowing the love of Christ, which is beyond all knowledge", we are "filled with the utter fullness of God" (*Ephesians 3:18, 19*).

Suggested Scripture reading

Old Testament: 2 Kings 22—25; Jeremiah 1—45; Isaiah 40—55. New Testament: The Epistle to the Ephesians.

6   God as lover

For till I am substantially oned to him,
I may never have full rest nor very bliss:
that is to say, till I be so fastened to him,
that there is right nought that is made
betwixt my God and me.
The Cloud of Unknowing

One of the most daring pictures of God to emerge from the Bible is that of husband and lover. But is it so strange, after all, since this is the most intimate of human relationships? If, as we have seen so often, the people of Israel looked to their own experiences in their search for a way of speaking about God, surely the one that was nearest to man's heart would eventually come to mind: "The heart speaks a language the mind does not understand."

Israel was at first reluctant to adopt the image of a husband to portray God's relationship with her. This was understandable in the light of the religious practices of the peoples among whom she lived. Their religions were, on the whole, "nature" religions, that is, their gods were seen as the source of the powers of nature, especially those of fertility. Fertility in earth, beast and man was thought to be brought about by the union of the god of fertility, Baal, with his consort, Astarte. If men were to share in this fertility, they must imitate ritually the union between the gods and so the practice of sacred prostitution was widespread in all the "high places" of Baal worship.

The temptation to see God meeting them in the persons of these fertility gods was a very real one for the Israelites. If they were to integrate into the farming communities surrounding them they would take over the farming fertility rites. Not to do so must have been as hazardous for an ancient farmer as for a modern one to presume on a bumper crop without using fertilizers. And, of course, many Israelites yielded to the temptation and thought they were fulfilling their religious duties by worshipping God under the form of these fertility rites.

For a long time, therefore, leaders in Israel were slow to use the spouse image in connection with God. The first to do so was the prophet Hosea in the eighth century BC. It was a risk, but it certainly paid dividends, as it revealed to the people aspects of God of which they would otherwise have been completely unaware.

Hosea and Gomer

Hosea's insight came directly from his own experience of marriage to Gomer, a woman who became a prostitute, but whom he continued to love deeply and was willing to take back, even if her only motive for returning might be security in old age. With a heart made sensitive by this searing experience and with the deep forgiveness he was prepared to show towards Gomer, he gradually realised that this was exactly the kind of relationship that God had with his people, a people who were forever proving unfaithful to him but whom he loved, nevertheless, with that same almost irrational foolishness of love that Hosea had felt himself:

> O Israel! Why have you pierced my heart
> Why have you gone? . . .
> How can I forget that I have made you
> Given you my life and love,
> Promised you my heart? . . .
> O Israel! How can I keep you back
> And make you mine?
> I will heal the wounds inflicted on you,
> Comfort I will bring to you;
> Tender is my heart. . . .
> Will you return to me
> And be my bride?
> I shall make you mine, my love, forever;
> Give me back your faithful love;
> Give me back your heart.

This beautiful modern hymn-version of Hosea's insight into God's love, brings out very poignantly what is, perhaps, the most profound paradox of the Bible: God's love for man, a love which urges him to pursue us and not to take "No" for an answer, even though he is rebuffed over and over again. We can imagine a God who is a ruler, a saviour, even a father; but one who is a lover is something that is too much for us.

And yet, what if it were true? What if, in spite

of all our infidelities, it were true that our God is a God who loves us? We would not want to accept it! How else can we explain the total lack of understanding on the part of Israel, and on our own part, for this offer of love?

To accept love, one has to have open hands and an open heart. Most of us are completely incapable of this and the story of the Bible is one long litany of instances showing such lack of openness. It is summed up in the Gospel story of the rich young man who turned away sad, because his fists were tightly clenched around his possessions.

This sadness at not being able to respond to love is, perhaps, the real anguish of mankind and matches the sadness of God in not being able to get through to man. He has to sidetrack, double back on his tracks, find any and every way of making us come face to face with him. The knocks and jolts of life can be a means of doing this; very often someone who has suffered has a real insight into God. You can sometimes see it in a person's eyes. I remember once being struck by the eyes of a Carmelite nun; her face showed signs of deep suffering, but her eyes were those of a person who had seen God. The same day, I met a widow who had been on crutches for twenty-five years and who had very real family troubles; yet her life was full of an optimistic search for an even deeper encounter with God. We all know similar cases of people who have emerged from suffering to a deep realisation of the meaning of life, and who have met the living God in their hearts, whether they realise it or not.

"Knowing" God

There are saints of the Bible and of all ages, those great names we know about and the many, many others of whom we know nothing and who are still in our midst. These, when their hearts are fired with the love of God and their senses flooded to intoxication with that love, experience a longing to look upon God with their bodily eyes. They find themselves praying with the intensity of Moses in the desert longing to see the face of God (*Exodus 33:18–23*).

But how can the narrowness of human vision enclose God whom the whole world cannot hold? This is the paradox of love, the reason why Israel came to speak of God as lover: "Love knows nothing about judgment, is beyond reason and is incapable of moderation. Love takes no relief from the fact that its object is beyond possibility, nor is it cured by difficulties." These words from a writer of the early Christian centuries go as far as we are capable of going in trying to find an answer to the question of how we can come to know God. The answer will have to be an answer of the heart rather than of the mind and, therefore, will not be capable of rational proofs since the heart is not interested in rational proofs. As the *Cloud of Unknowing* puts it, in its quaint mediaeval English:

> By love alone can he be gotten and holden
> But by thinking never.

It is interesting, in this context, that the word "to know" in Hebrew denotes more than a purely intellectual knowledge. It is significant that it is the word used for marital intercourse, so it implies the complete giving over of the whole person to another. God's love, therefore, calls us to turn round on our heels, look him in the eyes, as it were, and give in to the fact that he loves us. "God must be allowed to surprise us", Paddy Kavanagh says in his poem: "After Confession". This is what conversion implies and this is what the prophets were forever asking Israel to do. But they, and we, are far more interested in doing things for God—building a temple maybe, capturing his enemies—than in turning round and facing him: "Pause awhile and know that I am God" (*Psalm 46:10*).

If we fail to turn round and face him, he will begin the chase all over again. Often in the Bible one can see this fresh initiative on God's part. We have seen something of it already in the uprooting of Israel for exile. Perhaps the most intense description of such a fresh start is in Jeremiah:

> See the days are coming—it is Yahweh who speaks—when I will make a new covenant with the House of Israel, but not a covenant like the one I made with their ancestors on the day I took them by the hand to bring them out of the land of Egypt. . . . No, this is the covenant I will make with the House of Israel. . . . Deep within them I will plant my Law, writing it in their hearts. Then I will be their God and they shall be my people. There will be no further need for neighbour to try to teach neighbour, or brother to say to brother,

"Learn to know Yahweh!" No, they will all
know me, the least no less than the greatest . . .
since I will forgive their iniquity and never
call their sin to mind (*Jeremiah 31:31–34*).

As we saw earlier, the Israelites looked on their
original meeting with God in the desert, as a
marriage covenant. But Israel had been unfaithful
to the covenant of her youth. So now God renews
the covenant with her, no longer written on
stone, as the ten commandments were, but on her
heart. In passing, it is interesting to remark that
some Christian couples are now speaking of the
marriage bond as a covenant rather than as a con-
tract, since the latter has too much of the connotations of a business deal.

Fidelity

Fidelity in marriage can be a striking picture
of what God's fidelity to us is like, but is not a
sterile turned-in-on-itself type of fidelity. Caryl
Houslander, in one of her books, has given a
graphic description of what married love is *not*;
the picture is drawn from the kind of language we
sometimes use to portray our love of God:

Now it is impossible to imagine anyone in any
human relationship enduring, let alone being
pleased by, the things we do to please God!
This can only be realised by imagining the very
same things in a profound human relationship. . . . Picture to yourself a husband and
wife. . . . With averted eyes and hanging head
she advances and offers him a sheet of paper.

"List of the little things I have done today
which may offend you: I spilt a drop of milk.
I folded your shirt a little carelessly. I allowed
my mind to wander from the thought of you
twice while preparing your dinner. I allowed
a shirt button to remain under the chest of
drawers and bought another to replace it." . . .
She produces another paper and he reads.
"Pinpricks provoked for you today: Pricked my
finger on purpose while darning your socks.
Refrained from turning on the radio. Ate
nauseating cheap lunch. Allowed the baby to
cry all day without stopping."

The picture is a caricature of a certain type of
confession which is less frequent now than it used
to be, but it can still tell us something of the nig-
gardly way we can approach God's love. His fidelity
towards us, on the other hand, is a creative fidelity,
the "letting-be" of creation, which we spoke about
earlier, and so ours, too, must have something of
that joyous creativity which one can see in a true
marriage relationship where the partners help to
build one another up, making each other more
truly human in the process of growing closer to
one another.

The bridegroom comes

The Old Testament, therefore, saw God as a
husband, and Christ when he came, was not slow
to speak of himself as the bridegroom (cf. *Matthew
9:15*). His uncompromising attitude to divorce
maintains this idea of the enduring fidelity of
God's love in spite of our infidelity. The person

who is truly Christian will, like Hosea, come to realise the meaning of God's love through his own enduring fidelity, in spite of the complete withdrawal of the other person. No-one will deny that this is a difficult vocation and Christ was the first to show his concern for people in marital troubles: his treatment of the woman taken in adultery (*John 8*), and the Samaritan woman at the well (*John 4*), bear this out. At the same time, his ideal remains very high in this, as in every other area of life.

The Cross shows how Christ himself lived out this ideal; it clearly demonstrates God's love and the lengths he was prepared to go to in order to win his bride for himself:

> This is the love I mean:
> not our love for God,
> but God's love for us when he sent his Son
> to be the sacrifice that takes our sins away.
> My dear people,
> since God has loved us so much,
> we too should love one another (*1 John 4:9–11*).

Suggested Scripture reading

Old Testament: The Book of Hosea. New Testament: First Epistle of John.

7 Singing of God

*If you keep a green bough in your heart
the singing bird will come*

Chinese proverb

Is it any wonder, then, that the mystics of all
religions use the language of the love relationship
between man and woman to try to express something of the love between God and man? The
Bible shows the way with its beautiful song of love
called, interestingly enough, the *Song of Songs*.
Love seems to bring out the best (and the worst)
in music. The fact that this love song escaped the
censors among the men who put the Bible together
is surely proof that the Holy Spirit had a hand in
preserving the contents of the Bible! Because it
really is nothing if not a sensuous singing of the
joy of human love.

The *Song of Songs* came to be interpreted as
singing of the love between God and Israel and,
as such, it presents one of the most daring illustrations of God in the Bible: no longer the sober
and saddened husband, waiting for his faithless
wife to return to him, he is now the young lover
wildly excited at the prospect of being with his
beloved, murmuring foolish things in her ear under

the apple blossoms, turning her heart and her head until she can think of nothing but him:

> You ravish my heart
> my sister, my promised bride,
> you ravish my heart
> with a single one of your glances,
> with one single pearl of your necklace
> (*Song of Songs 4:9–10*).

It is as vivid a picture as one could dare imagine of God's pursuit of us.

Longing for God

There are other songs in the Bible, of course; there is the *Book of Psalms* for instance. The word "psalm" basically means a song, a song from the heart answering God's call to us for our love. The intense thirst of the heart of man for God can be seen especially in the following psalm:

> God, my God, I look for you.
> All I am is thirst for you.
> My body is a land without water,
> exhausted with desire for you. . . .
>
> I stretch out my hands to you,
> I call your Name—you are my God,
> my daily bread, life in abundance—
> I will never tire of singing of you
> (*Psalm 63, Fifty Psalms* version).

Just as a person can "fall in love" suddenly, out of the blue, without knowing why, so the realisation of God's love for us can be a dramatic and unexpected thing. The deeper the experience, the more ardent the longing for his return, a longing which can only find expression in the groanings of the human spirit. The depths of man call out to be filled by the depths of God (cf. *Psalm 130*). In *Romans,* Saint Paul speaks of this longing, a longing in which he sees the whole of creation involved, as of someone in an attitude of waiting, with his neck eagerly thrust forward, peering into the far distance (*Romans 8:23*).

It is in this context that we can understand the upsurge of Pentecostal prayer, especially that of speaking in tongues. There has always been this fundamental need in the human spirit to give expression to the deep desire that is within us for God. But, for most people, this lies buried beneath so many layers of fear, of worry, or whatever, that it never sees the daylight at all! As Peter Hocken in *You He Made Alive* has put it:

> The prayer of tongues is the Spirit activating in us in our worship of God a natural capacity for non-conceptual expression. Part of the inadequacy of our language for the praise of God is that normal human language operates through the formation of images and concepts; and when the majesty and glory of God sweep us up, our minds somehow get in the way! It is then that the prayer of tongues, which expresses the human spirit in sound and song by-passing the mediation of the mind, comes to our aid. From the nature of the case, anyone whose prayer has become predominantly the prayer of praise is near to praying in tongues. . . .

Shouts of praise

The spontaneous reaction of a lover is to praise the beloved; to say how beautiful are her eyes, her hair and so on. So the spontaneous reaction of the psalmist to the realisation of God's love is to praise him. The psalms of praise are shouts of pure joy at the realisation that God is God, with all that this means to us. The expressive word, Alleluia, which often opens these psalms of praise, is one of those shouts of intense joy. Used, as it often is today, as a catch-word to sum up the aspiration of the human heart towards God, it can give meaning too to all one would like to say, if only one had the words to express oneself.

Sharing is part of the essence of such spontaneous outbursts; joy loses all meaning if it cannot communicate itself. There is an interesting difference here between joy and sorrow: sorrow can be borne patiently alone, even if it is very deep and even when it would help enormously to have someone to share it; but joy cannot be kept to oneself. It must find expression somehow.

Little children can bring this home to us most refreshingly. I remember once being accosted on a lonely beach by a six-year-old, as I was coming in from a swim. I had never met the boy before but I was at least a person to talk to, and without as much as a "Hello, who are you?" he began to show me the pinkeens he had caught in his pail and to share blissfully the whole drama of the catch.

It is because of this element of shared joy that the psalms of praise have always been used by the Church in its worship and used by all denomina-

tions when they pray together. Because they speak
much more with the language of the heart than
with the neat definitions of the head, they express
human emotions in prayer in a way that has never
been surpassed. *Psalm 150,* the last of the biblical
group of psalms, sums them all up in a vibrant
symphony of praise to God:

> Praise the Lord in his holy house,
> the firmament of his majesty.
> Praise him for his powerful works,
> praise him, he is immeasurably great.
> Praise him with resounding horns,
> and with your lutes and harps and guitars.
> Praise him with dancing and tambourines,
> tune your strings and play the flute.
> Praise him with kettledrums and cymbals,
> brass and woodwind, a choir of voices,
> alleluia, shouts of joy,
> all the living are praising the Lord
> (*Fifty Psalms* version).

Up to the neck in hot water (cf. *Psalm* 69:1)

But joy is not the only human emotion that we
find in the psalms. Sorrow is there too and, mirror-
ing human life, there is far more sorrow than joy.
No collection of human songs would be complete
without those which take in the areas of human
misery, depression and failure. There are the obvious experiences of sickness and disease and the fear
of death, which call forth a cry from the heart for
their remedy. The whole question of suffering,
especially that of innocent suffering, was a great
problem for the Jews since their religion for many

centuries held to the belief that the good would be rewarded and the wicked punished. This had to be done in the here-and-now. Their way of thinking of the after-life cut out any notion of a reward. They believed that, after death, the person went to "Sheol" which was a mere twilight existence where one was only a shade of one's former self and where one could not know God, or be happy.

Cursing psalms

At times this frustration with suffering comes through in the psalms as a tirade against those who have caused the suffering, usually wealthy enemies who are looked on as hounding the poor:

> That wretch never thought of being kind,
> but hounded the poor, the needy
> and the broken-hearted to death.
> He loved cursing, may it recoil on him,
> had no taste for blessing, may it shun him!
> He used to wrap curses round him like a cloak,
> let them soak right into him like water,
> deep into his bones like oil. . . .
> (*Psalm 109:16–18*).

We can be shocked by such downright vindictiveness in a religious song and we are not meant to see it as a right attitude. Why then include these psalms in the songs of the Church at all? This question has often been asked and, as a matter of fact, the particular psalm quoted above has been omitted from the breviary, the Church's official prayer book. I think this is a pity, because what

c

we have here is a spontaneous reaction to discrimination. Christianity, it is true, has gone beyond the vindictiveness of earlier times and asks us to love our enemies. But what these psalms can at least do is to draw our attention to the existence of evil in our world, to the racial and other discrimination that is going on all around us and in which we too may be sharing, and to the presence of organised evil, for example in drug or alcohol pushing, which is ruining the lives of so many young people. Reading such psalms can alert us to the frustration of those who suffer from injustice of any kind, and spur us on to come to their defence.

Besides the psalms there is in the Bible another poetic exploration of this problem of innocent suffering. The author of the *Book of Job* gives us the most caustic picture of God found in the Bible:

> Will you never take your eyes off me
> long enough for me to swallow my spittle?
> Suppose I have sinned, what have I done to you,
> You tireless watcher of mankind?
> (*Job 7:19, 20*).

We are familiar with the saying, "the patience of Job", but Job was the most impatient of men as he tried to come to an understanding of human suffering. We are familiar too with his friends, "Job's comforters", who come to console him but who only add insult to injury by trotting out pious platitudes which do not reach the depths of his misery. We have all experienced this with people in time of need: no amount of high-sounding words will reach them. What they need most of all at such times is the quiet presence and sympathy of another person.

The pious talk of his friends only drives Job on to further extremes of questioning as he rails against the way he sees God ruling the world. For Job, the problem of innocent suffering is taken up into the larger problem of man's relationship with God. Why are God's ways with man so inscrutable? Why does God not intervene to save the innocent? Where is the justice of God? In grappling with the problem, Job who often saw God as tormentor and aggressor, now appeals to him as saviour. He is not logical in his thought but in his groping he breaks through the narrow idea of God which is that proffered by his friends. It is through the questioning of Job, rather than through the safe orthodoxy of the friends that a deeper understanding of God is reached. Not that Job, or the psalmists, get answers to their questions! We are given a picture of God coming to meet Job "out of the whirlwind" and in this meeting Job realises that God is too "big" for man to understand. Failing to understand, he is willing to leave everything in God's hands, realising something of what man is before his creator.

In the meeting with God, Job's one blind spot was cured. For in his former protestations of innocence and upright behaviour he had shown himself the worthy forerunner of the Pharisee who later said, "I am not like the rest of men". He had been too blind to see that "None is good save God alone". Suffering had matured him, had helped him to see that there are depths of darkness and uncleanness in man before a God who is a "devouring fire" where sin is concerned. Confessing his rashness, he finds himself in his repentance in a new relationship with God, the living God.

Living in sin

The awareness of sin is an even deeper misery for man than physical suffering. There are times when we come face to face with the realisation that even our best acts are flawed by sin, as we saw in the chapter on Adam and Eve. We are all of us "living in sin", though not necessarily in the way that phrase has come to be interpreted in an Irish context, where immorality tends to be equated with sexual deviation.

We all need the healing words of *Psalm 51* :

> Have mercy on me, O God, in your goodness,
> in your great tenderness wipe away my faults;
> wash me clean of my guilt,
> purify me from my sin . . .
> God, create a clean heart in me,
> put into me a new and constant spirit,
> do not banish me from your presence,
> do not deprive me of your holy spirit.

Evil is not just all around us; it is in us too. There is a passage in Solzhenitsyn's book on Russian prison life, *The Gulag Archipelago,* which brings this out very strongly. He has been describing the excesses of the Russian secret security men, and shows how in prison he has come to the realisation that the division between good people and bad is not as simple as we can make it appear:

If only there were evil people somewhere in-
sidiously committing evil deeds and it were
necessary only to separate them from the rest
of us and destroy them. But the line dividing
good and evil cuts right through the heart of
every human being. And who is willing to
destroy a piece of his own heart?

We need to be renewed in heart over and over
again, and life will bring us face to face with such
renewal in the most unusual ways. This is another
dimension to the problem of innocent suffering:
there is no greater way of refining our insensitive
natures.

The answer to the problem of innocent suffering, therefore, is largely left unsolved in the Old
Testament. But in the reassertion of the relationship of man with God by faith, a deeper dimension
is revealed. For the Christian, this dimension is
deepened immeasurably, because when he meets
his God, it is no longer a God speaking "out of
the whirlwind" in power and majesty but one who,
though innocent, took man's sufferings on himself:

Being as all men are
He was humbler yet
Even to accepting death
Death on a cross (*Philippians 2:8*).

Suggested Scripture reading
*Old Testament: The Song of Songs; Psalms 63,
42–43 (longing for God); 8, 19, 95, 104, 111–116
(praise); 7, 22, 38, 51, 69, 130 (in times of distress);
The Book of Job. New Testament: Colossians
1:15–20; Philippians 2:6–11.*

8 Meeting God in man

The gospels don't lay down the law.
They aren't an assertion: "It's like this
and like that." The gospels are an offer,
a naïve and diffident offer: "Would you like
to live in a completely new way?"
Pasternak *Dr Zhivago*

Coming from the Old Testament into the New is
like the change-over from using black and white
stills to a high-powered colour cine film. Up to
this we have, as it were, got flashes in the dark,
but all our insights needed the fullness of God's
revelation of himself in Christ to be complete. In
him we are given a real clue as to what God is like
and his way of acting in our world.

In the baby in the crib, the wandering preacher
and miracle-worker with his call to brotherly love,
peace and joy, the criminal dying on the Cross in
anguish and yet victorious, we meet the image of
the God who gives life and gives himself in a way
that should jolt us out of our hard-heartedness. We
have long ago taken the brutality out of our cruci-
fixes, and the crib has become a cosy, tinselly place.
But we should focus on the reality of what Christ's
life really was in order to come to grips with the
kind of insight into God which his coming has
meant.

For the people who met him, the scandal of Jesus lay in his claim that the inaccessible and holy God was close and near to us. But, for us, the real scandal is that he should become close and near to us in such a way: through the weakness, failure and death of a human being.

Jesus in his times

It is through the human life of Jesus therefore that we must see God at work—from the inside out, as it were, in and through the very ordinary experiences of human life. To meet Jesus was to be invited, without knowing it to a personal encounter with the living God. We have tended to think of him as living in a kind of a vacuum, floating serenely around the Palestine of his time, touching down now and then to work a miracle or two, or to utter some wise saying which would be carefully preserved for posterity. Instead we must be prepared to see his real humanness; to see him growing up and coming to an understanding of human life, in a way any ordinary Jewish boy would. He was immersed in the Jewish background of his times, learning to think, to pray and to come to an understanding of the will of his Father from the Bible, from the people among whom he lived and from all that was happening in the Jewish life around him.

His was a life lived against the odds of tremendous pressures; pressure from religious leaders to conform to the accepted ways of looking at God and the Law; pressure from extremists to bring about the new radical society in their way of viol-

ence and bloodshed; pressure from ordinary people
to be a popular leader. These pressures were very
real in his life. Yet he remained free, and searched
out the meaning of his mission from the Father.
The story of the temptations in the desert shows
that more spectacular alternatives to the way of
suffering suggested themselves to him. It was by
trial and effort, therefore, that he discovered the
best way to bring about the Father's will, which
was to preach a basic call to repentance asking
people to turn round and opt again for the Father's
love; to really take seriously that their God was a
God of love and not some type of stern judge as
the Pharisees argued, with their insistence on strict
accountancy with him.

Jesus for our times

It is in the gospels that we are brought face to
face with this coming of God in the person of
Christ. The message of Christ stands out as clearly
as a cross against the skyline but we become so
used to it that we tend to be blind and deaf to its
impact. We all need to reinterpret the Gospel in
our own language and culture in order to see its
meaning for ourselves. It will generally be out of
our own experience that we do this.

This truth was brought home to me in a striking
way once, when I was taking part in a Bible study
group. The people there, mainly young married
couples, began simply and honestly to examine
how the Sermon on the Mount cut right through
many of the structures of their lives which they
had always taken for granted: structures of power,

of comfort, of lack of honesty. The Sermon on the Mount is not a set of laws which bind us to a minimum, but a call on the part of Christ drawing us on towards the fullness of the life to which the Father's love is calling us. He overthrows the values we take for granted, values of wealth, power, even religion if it is conceived in the too narrow way of the Pharisees. The honesty and sincerity of these Christians facing up to the demands of Christ out of their own experience was a tremendous example to me who had lived and worked with the Bible for so long that perhaps it had become over-familiar. Out of the confrontation between their experience and the Gospel, I too was brought face to face in a very vivid and penetrating way with the demands of Christ in my own situation.

This is the benefit of any kind of sharing of our faith. We are rediscovering the meaning of Christ's words: "Where two or three meet in my name, I shall be there with them" (*Matthew 18:20*). We become the eyes, ears and mouth of Christ to one another as we give witness to the need that is in us for God, and to our own experience of him. And, of course, this must lead to action for others if we are to be true to the one who gave himself that we "may have life and have it to the full" (*John 10:10*).

Our spontaneous impulse to care and help tells us something about the kind of God we are dealing with, as Christ pointed out in the parable of the Good Samaritan (*Luke 10:29–37*). Leading up to this parable is the lawyer's question: "Master, what must I do to inherit eternal life?", followed by Jesus' reply about loving God with all one's being and one's neighbour as oneself. To the further question "Who is my neighbour?", Jesus does not give the abstract general reply we are familiar with from the Catechism: "My neighbour is all mankind. . . ." He answers far more convincingly with the story of the Good Samaritan, the point of which is obvious: when you see someone in need, help him. But if we are like this picture of our Father, we will go out of our way, putting ourselves to the endless trouble of being anxious that a needy person is cared for. This is the meaning behind Christ's saying: "If anyone gives so much as a cup of cold water to one of these little ones. . . ."; cold water was difficult to come by in a hot land like Palestine where there were no fridges, so a good deal of trouble would be involved in procuring some. In our climate the equivalent would be to boil the kettle and treat the person to a cup of hot tea!

The cross of the world

It is when we come to the Cross that we see Christ himself acting out the parable of the Good Samaritan. The Cross is the point of departure for our faith, for the realisation of what God's love in action means for us. The Cross does not give us a picture of a God who demands the slaughter of his innocent son to pacify his wrath with the rest of mankind. This would be a very pagan picture of God. The Cross shows us what happens when a God of love decides to identify with his creatures, and in so doing gives himself into their power:

"Anyone who has stretched his existence so wide that he is simultaneously immersed in God and in the depths of the God-forsaken creature is bound to be torn asunder, as it were; such a one is truly crucified" (Ratzinger *Introduction to Christianity*). Many of us will have experienced the agony of trying to bring about a reconciliation whether it is between members of a family, of a group, or between two warring factions of society, as in the North of Ireland. Having a hand in both sides can be a real experience of being torn asunder, of being crucified.

We must see in the Cross, then, how far Christ actually went in his identification with us in pain, frustration, failure and death. We must see him brought right to the edge of despair, to a feeling of complete abandonment by his Father, so that there is a very real sense in which Jesus was the first one for whom the term, "the death of God", became a reality. He became a stranger to the Father and, while still retaining his tremendous trust in the Father, he experienced in his person mankind's deepest darkness: its alienation from God. It is a sobering thought for us, and the realisation that we can be the cause of this death of God in other people must make it all the more real to us. As the Vatican Council put it:

> Believers are to blame
> if by their evident failings
> they hide God's face from the world
> when they should be showing it.
> (*The Church in the Modern World,* Grail version)

Life through death

If the Cross means anything it means that we must
see life as coming through death:

> Unless a wheat grain falls on the ground
>   and dies,
> it remains only a single grain;
> but if it dies,
> it yields a rich harvest (*John 12:24*).

Here we have the whole paradox of Christian living. The Cross of Christ continually calls us to die
to the selfishness in us, if we are to be transformed
into life with him. This is what resurrection means.

We are all called to share in Christ's reconciliation. The dying demanded of us here will vary
with different people. For one it will be in the
daily monotony of the constant giving in love,
which bringing up a family demands; for another
it will be in the gruelling effort of creative work.
For some it will be brought about in the martyrdom of physical or mental suffering; for others in
the responsibilities entrusted to them by their
fellow men. It is not usually in the cross we choose
for ourselves, therefore, that we learn to share with
Christ, but in the suffering and agony, perhaps,
that life brings our way. But then, what has
ripened throughout life in the gift of oneself, and
what seemed to us only a dying, will surely not
perish. It will be transformed with Christ into the
resurrected life.

We should already be spreading around us this
joy of the resurrection because Christ has already
risen and is already making us share in the new

life. I once heard a charismatic speaker say that we Christians were very good at spreading information about the death of Jesus but not so good at giving witness to the joy of the resurrection. There are people who prefer the darkness of self-imposed martyrdom and misery to the joyous light which the resurrection brings. A passage in Iris Murdoch's novel, *The Red and the Green,* illustrates this point very well. The central character, Barney, has made a mess of his life: he tried the priesthood but left because of an infatuation. Unable to relate to his over-pious wife, he has become a hopeless alcoholic. He finds he can identify very well with the Christ of Good Friday, but on Easter Sunday morning, he suddenly realises that, if he is to be saved from himself, this is not enough; he must also accept the joy of the risen Christ and he knows in his heart that he does not want to do this.

Few of us are as honest as Barney in realising our slowness to accept the light of the risen Christ. Unless we do, however, we will never come to the fullness of joy which should be ours as a result of the Cross.

When this light breaks through to us, in however fragile a way, there can only be one response: Lord, remain with us—the response of the two forlorn disciples on the road to Emmaus (*Luke 24:13–35*). Their hearts, like ours often are, were so heavy at the seeming finality of death, that their eyes were held from recognising Christ alive and in their midst again. Significantly enough, it was in the sharing of their bread with this apparent stranger that they became conscious of who was with them. It is true that in sharing what we have with others we will come to a deeper understanding of Christ's presence among us:

> My prayer is that your love for each other may increase more and more and never stop improving your knowledge and deepening your perception so that you can always recognise what is best (*Philippians 1:11*).

Suggested Scripture reading
The Gospel of Luke.

9   Living with God

I don't know who—or what—put the question,
I don't know when it was put.
I don't even remember answering,
But at some moment, I did answer Yes
to Someone—or Something—
and from that hour I was certain
that existence is meaningful and that,
therefore, my life, in self surrender, had a goal.
Dag Hammarskjold *Markings*

Saint Paul's epistles are alive with the early
Christians' exuberant rediscovery of God after he
had been buried beneath, on the one hand, men's
grasping greed in a time of empire building and,
on the other, the Pharisee's minute regulations of
religious book-keeping. Both these attitudes were
attacked again and again by Christ and eventually
were the cause of his death. Paul, perhaps his
most enthusiastic follower ever, carried on the fight
in the cosmopolitan world of his time. It was a
world that had much in common with our own,
in its anguished search for meaning in the midst
of a general breakdown of morals and values.

Man in sin

Paul was realistic about mankind's sinful condition. As we have seen, we are all well aware of the environment of sin in which we live. Exploiting the widow, the orphan, the stranger and the old did not happen only in the ancient world; it is still very much with us, even in the Welfare State. While writing this, I came upon a newspaper article headed: *The Most Cruel Racket of Them All*, which described how a New Yorker had become a multimillionaire by providing nursing homes for the old. Keeping the old people in most appalling conditions, he pocketed the money supplied by the State for their benefit, and the whole proceedings appeared perfectly legal!

But none of us can point the finger. A look at how Paul speaks of man in sin may cause us some shocks. Basically, he sees sin as the selfish attitude of turning in on ourselves rather than being open to others. Wherever he gives a list of sins they are always a list of anti-social actions:

> When self-indulgence is at work the results are obvious: fornication, gross indecency and sexual irresponsibility; idolatry and sorcery; feuds and wrangling, jealousy, bad temper and quarrels; disagreements, factions, envy; drunkenness, orgies and similar things (*Galatians 5:19–20*).

It is interesting to note that there is no grading of sins here. Bad temper and quarrels are mentioned in the same breath as gross indecency and sexual irresponsibility. For Paul it is all sin.

A look at the words he uses can be instructive: as we might expect, he speaks of arrogance and boasting to express the selfish self-reliance that sin is. But we may be surprised to see him also condemning attitudes like care and fear. What he means is the over-anxious concern for one's own welfare, the taking out of an insurance policy on the Lord, as it were, so as to guarantee one's spiritual future. Religion is not an insurance policy; if we are not ready to take risks, we may find ourselves very far from God indeed:

> There is in the human heart a deep thirst for risk. All of us have this thirst, and the day we no longer take risks, something will have died within us (Vanier *Eruption to Hope*).

Man in Christ

The Christian, therefore, is called on to make an enthusiastic choice of God as he has shown himself to us in Christ. Paul could speak of himself as "Christ's man", ready to do what God's interests demanded of him in the situations of his life. It is this whole-hearted response to God in Christ, with no strings attached, that we, too, must aim at if we are to be true followers of Christ.

This is what faith is all about. It is not just giving a notional assent to a set of truths. Paul sees it as a process which begins by hearing and ends up as a personal commitment to God in Christ. In between, we must learn to discern the actions which will really help us to follow out this commitment:

> Spiritual discernment is the process of sifting through the felt needs and desires, the spontaneous impulses and inclinations, the con-

flicting interior reactions that we experience when we confront the situations and events of our lives in order to separate the "wheat" of those that move us to choose loving actions from the "chaff" of those that move us to choose selfish ones (J. C. Futrell *The Way,* October 1971).

It was at baptism that we were brought into this relationship with God in Christ. But since baptism came to most of us when we were babies, we have perhaps never faced up to its reality. It should really be for all of us the beginning of a new life. This was to be seen much more clearly in the early Church where the font was in the nature of a bath set into the ground. One went down steps on one side becoming completely immersed in the water and then came up on the other side. This symbolised going down into death with Christ in order to come to resurrection with him. As Paul put it:

> You have been taught that when we were baptised into Christ Jesus, we were baptised into his death; in other words, when we were baptised we went into the tomb with him and joined him in death; so that as Christ was raised from the dead by the Father's glory we too might live a new life (*Romans 6:3, 4*).

The Easter Vigil ceremony of the renewal of baptismal promises should be for us a genuine facing up again to our commitment to Christ and a glad response to the demands this makes on our lives. This is also what is involved in the Pentecostal "Baptism in the Spirit". It is not another baptism but a release of the effects of our initial baptism in our lives, as we come to a fuller understanding of that sacrament.

Being and becoming

Paul was well aware of the gap between what we are called to be and what we really are. He often speaks in glowing terms of the faith of his converts, of their wonderful new condition in Christ and, in the next breath, gives them a good dressing down because their actual practice gives the lie to what they profess to be. Take his letter to the Church in Corinth, for instance. The Corinthians had received the faith with great enthusiasm and Paul acknowledges how far they have come:

> I never stop thanking God for all the graces you have received through Jesus Christ. I thank him that you have been enriched in so many ways, especially in your teachers and preachers; the witness to Christ has indeed been strong among you . . . (*1 Corinthians 1:4, 5*).

But Paul then goes on to show up the ways in which they are falsifying the faith:

> All the same I do appeal to you, brothers, for the sake of our Lord Jesus Christ, to make up the differences between you and instead of disagreeing among yourselves, to be united again in your belief and practice (*1:10, 11*).

Even though they prided themselves on having great wisdom and knowledge of God and had received many gifts and charisms (such as speaking in tongues), Paul says he can only think of them as babies in the faith, still at the milk stage and not nearly ready yet for strong meat (*3:1–4*).

What the Corinthians had to learn, and what we too find so difficult, is that though the commitment to Christ is a very personal thing and growth in this commitment demands the use of all the talents and graces God has given us, yet our attention is not to be directed inward, towards our own development but outward to the needs of others. This is one of Paul's deepest insights. He who had God's image so deeply imprinted on himself, through his complete surrender to Christ, wished he could produce in his converts innumerable copies of this self-giving God with whom he had come face to face. Again and again, therefore, he gave them pointers to the kind of attitude which being in Christ calls for.

Freedom

The way he talks about freedom is one such pointer. For Paul, this is a freedom from sin (from living for oneself) in order to be free for Christ and for one's fellow man (cf. *2 Corinthians 5:15* ff.): that is, I no longer belong to myself; no longer have the care for myself but must put myself at the service of the living God and in so doing become the "slave of all".

Freedom is "being obliged", as one present-day philosopher put it. This can make strenuous demands on a person, and Paul's converts, like all of us, wanted freedom without any of the obligations. There is the example, for instance, of the liberal-minded Christians who had no pangs of conscience about eating meat which had been sacrificed to idols. Seeing this, their more scrupulous brothers were in danger of sinning since they followed their example even though they felt guilty about it. Paul said he was just as free to eat as the most liberal-minded, yet he would never eat meat again if by doing so he would be the cause of the downfall of one of his fellow Christians:

> Far from passing judgment on each other, therefore, you should make up your mind never to be the cause of your brother tripping or falling. ... So let us adopt any custom that leads to peace and our mutual improvement (*Romans 14:13, 15, 19*).

We may not have the same problems as the early Christians but Paul's principle will apply wherever the good of others comes in the way of our freedom. The choice is clear-cut. Freedom is not a question of doing what I like or what appeals to my feelings or good taste. It means seeking out the inner challenge of a situation in the light of my total commitment to Christ.

Love

For Paul, therefore, love of others is real only in service. It is based on the realisation that God loved us first and showed that love in the giving of himself to us (cf. *Romans 5:8*). Our response to

that love is spelt out in practical terms in his in-
spired hymn to love (*1 Corinthians 13*). It is a
sharing in the joys and sorrows of others:

> Love is always patient and kind; it is never
> jealous;

It shows forgiveness even of enemies:

> Love is never boastful or conceited; it is never
> rude or selfish; it does not take offence and is
> not resentful.

It is ready to go to any lengths for another:

> Love takes no pleasure in other people's sins
> but delights in the truth; it is always ready to
> excuse, to trust, to hope and to endure what-
> ever comes.

A true Christian is one who has learned to love
like this and for Paul, such love is the only basis
for a Christian community.

All the time, therefore, our values and standards
have to be judged in the light of Christ. Left to
ourselves, our basic attitude towards others will be
that of fear and jealousy and we will erect all sorts
of protective barriers. This is true of our own
society no less than of Paul's. A glance through a
book like Vance Packard's *The Status Seekers,*
gives devastating proof of this. There is the case,
for example, of the Holywood technician who got
promotion in his job. Immediately a barrier was
created between himself and his former compan-
ions. They could no longer mix socially because
the higher payroll man had to associate with his
new equals and live up to his new status.

There were plenty of barriers in Paul's time also, between Jew and non-Jew, Greek and barbarian, slave and freeman, men and women. Paul shows Christ as the great breaker-down of barriers; there is no place in the Christian Church for divisions of race, status, or sex and yet even within the Church we tend to set up barriers against one another, abiding by the principle so cryptically condemned by Robert Frost: "Good walls make good neighbours."

Christian community

Christ is the one who reconciles men to himself and to one another and we must show this reconciliation by being the type of Christian community where it will be seen to work. People today are tired of words; they want to see reconciliation in action and this is what we as Christians are called to. "See how these Christians love one another," it was said of the early Christians. Could it be said so readily of us?

The coming together in Christ of the early Christians made great demands on their faith: how stupid it was after all to stake all one had on a man who had been crucified as a criminal and was now supposed to be risen from the dead! There were times when they must really have felt the "foolishness of the Cross" as Paul called it (*1 Corinthians 1:24, 25*). Therefore they needed the warm, human, self-giving, supportive love of one another; Paul was the first to give this to each of his converts, so he knew what he was demanding of them:

Like a mother feeding and looking after her own children, we felt so devoted and protective towards you, and had come to love you so much, that we were eager to hand over to you not only the Good News but our whole lives as well (*1 Thessalonians 2:7, 8*).

It is not because we are called a Christian Church, family, or community, that we really are so; we have to be for ever on the alert to see if we are really Christian at heart, if we are trying to live up to the very demanding call of the Christian message. If we are not, which will most often be the case, then we must be prepared to renew ourselves over and over again according to the standards of the Cross and not according to those of our own times.

Suggested Scripture reading
Romans, 1 and 2 Corinthians.

10 God, first and last

> *We thank thee who has moved us to building,*
> *to finding, to forming at the ends of our*
> *fingers and beams of our eyes. . . .*
> *And we thank thee that darkness*
> *reminds us of light.*
> *O Light Invisible, we give thee thanks*
> *for thy great glory!*
> T. S. Eliot *The Rock*

"Abba, Father"

Things can never be the same again since Christ opened up the way to the Father for us. And, ultimately, this is the most revealing image of God: that we can look on him as a father. Because this was Christ's favourite way of showing us what God is like, we must make every effort to open our own experience to what he meant.

As we saw earlier, it was the picture of a tyrannical father which made the Israelites mistrust this image of God. However we know that Christ called him, "Abba", the Aramaic equivalent of our "Daddy", a term which no Jew of his time would have dreamed of using for God. Their image of him was still that of a remote lawgiver who could hardly be expected to condescend to a loving, not to say, playful relationship with his children.

Even though Jesus left us this way of addressing

the Father as our own, we tend to mistrust it. We accept in a general way that God is our loving Father but we find it difficult to apply this to ourselves. I must realise that God loves me and that I should have all the confidence in him that a little child has as it stretches out its tiny arms to its father and says, "Da-Da"! We must expect too that our Father will speak to us. Can we imagine a household in which the father never speaks to his children? And yet this is often our idea of God.

Christ once said: "He who sees me sees the Father" (*John 14:9*) and so, in all his words and actions we must see the Father at work. If Christ heals the sick, befriends sinners, if at the same time he can denounce hypocrisy in all its forms, then this must be the kind of attitude the Father has too.

The question has often been asked: "Where was the Father when Jesus was dying on the Cross?" If the image of God as Father is true, we must see him here as deeply involved. Jesus' saying: "He who has seen me has seen the Father", must be as true on Calvary as it was for the rest of his life. This is because the essence of fatherhood is just this: involvement with one's children.

We have all witnessed the agony a human father undergoes when his son is in trouble, and surely God's fatherhood can be no less than this. And if Jesus brings us to share his own sonship with the Father, then the Father is there for us too, and is deeply involved when we are in anguish and in doubt, even to the point of feeling completely cut off from him:

Everyone moved by the Spirit is a son of God. The spirit you received is not the spirit of slaves bringing fear into your lives again; it is the spirit of sons, and it makes us cry out, "Abba, Father!" The Spirit himself and our spirit bear united witness that we are children of God. And if we are children we are heirs as well: heirs of God and co-heirs with Christ, sharing his sufferings so as to share his glory (*Romans 8:14–17*).

Spirit of the living God

By speaking of God as Father, therefore, Jesus widened immeasurably our understanding of what God means. This is deepened still further by the insights of the early Church into the Spirit that Jesus seemed to have with him constantly in his life. A recent book by H. V. Taylor calls the Spirit the "Go-Between God". It is a book which makes fascinating reading as it traces the action of the Spirit in the whole of creation and in the life of Israel, before exploring his action in the Church. Taylor sees the same pattern emerging always: wherever you have true communication there you have the Spirit at work, anonymously as it were, because we can never perceive his action directly. He is the "go-between" in all our relationships, not only between God and man but also between one another.

It is the Spirit who brings us to a full awareness of life, suddenly lighting things up from within, as it were, until the patterns new and ever-changing, fall together as in a kaleidoscope. It is through the Spirit that we can "see" God's action—in the lilies of the field, the lost coin, the breaking of bread, or wherever it is in our own lives. But a great sensitivity, a sensitivity which Jesus had to a supreme degree, is needed in order to be alive to this "seeing".

It is the Spirit then who confronts us with opting for God in Christ, who urges us to take the plunge at the deep end of whatever new venture he is leading us to. Most of the time we are hesitating in fear at the brink of things. (This is the care against which Paul warned us.) So, too, it is the Spirit who leads us with Christ to the Cross, to the surrender that is necessary if we are to be free from ourselves so as to be free for Christ and others.

The results of the Spirit's action in our lives will gradually become visible to people around us when they see its fruit in our behaviour:

> What the Spirit brings is . . . love, joy, peace, patience, kindness, goodness, trustfulness, gentleness and self-control (*Galatians* 5:22).

In the early Church, marriage, celibacy, administrative gifts—from leadership down to service of others at table—were all regarded as gifts of the Spirit. But sometimes, too, more spectacular gifts may appear for the upbuilding of our fellow Christians. If anyone happens to have the more unusual gifts (for example, healing, speaking in tongues, or prophecy), he is not to take the glory to himself. The Spirit gives just as he wills, not for ourselves but for others (cf. *1 Corinthians 12—14*). Thus, we cannot say "no" lightly to the gifts of the Spirit and this is one of the values of the Charismatic Movement in the Church. It has reawakened us to accepting freely these gifts of the Spirit.

Likewise it is only in the Spirit that we can pray. And like the apostles in the upper room before Pentecost, we would do well to have our Lady with us when we pray, as no one was more sensitive than she to the presence of the Spirit in her life. There is a very expressive prayer of Simon Tugwell's which sums up Mary's place in our praying:

> May Mary, the mother of the Lord,
> pray with us
> as she did with those first disciples at Pentecost
> that upon us too the Holy Spirit may be
> poured out,
> the Spirit of wisdom and revelation,
> that, the eyes of our hearts being opened,
> we may know the hope of our calling
> and rejoice with unspeakable and holy joy,
> and speak with boldness the word of God.

Speaking with boldness the word of God

It is interesting that when the Spirit descended on the disciples at Pentecost, their first action was to praise and thank God. This praise so overflowed from the depths of their Spirit-filled hearts that many thought they were drunk, while others realised what was happening and were converted.

The praise came first, but the Spirit's coming always results sooner or later in communication. Pentecost has always been looked on as reversing what happened in the story of the tower of Babel in the Old Testament, where men had been scattered far and wide because of their sin.

The basic instinct of the Pentecostals, therefore, to praise and thank God for what he is in himself and for what he has done for us, is directly in line with the action of the Spirit in the early Church. It is a necessary reminder of what our attitude should be in the Church today—as long as we do not settle down merely to enjoy our praising in a self-centred way. The Spirit calls us to go out and share the riches we have received rather than hoard them up for ourselves.

This is what the mission of the Church is all about and, of course, it is *we* who are the Church. We must be prepared to pass on what we have received. As the Vatican Council puts it:

> The Church prays and labours
> so that the whole world may be transformed
> into the people of God,
> the body of the Lord,
> the temple of the Spirit,
> so that in Christ who is the head of everything
> all glory may be given
> to the Creator, Father of the Universe.
> (*Constitution on the Church*, *17*, Grail version)

God the future of man

While the world we live in has much that is dark and dreary about it, there is great cause for hope also in our faith. "Hope", as the Dutch Catechism has it, "is that aspect of faith which makes me certain that the world is cared for and loved by God." This opens us out in love towards the future, turning over our anxiety about ourselves and our world to God, anticipating nothing and ready to take the risk of trusting in him. This is not a "pie-in-the-sky" type of hope; it stirs us up here and now to work towards the fulfilment of creation. The work of Mother Teresa of Calcutta, of the various Christian programmes of development, such as Trócaire, Gorta, Christian Aid etc., point the way.

But it is not only a question of helping the Third World, however necessary this may be. The Christian revolution must touch us all in our ordinary everyday relationships if we are to show our belief in God as the future of mankind:

> Who could believe in God who will make everything new "later" if it is in no way apparent from the activity of those who hope in the One who is to come that he is already beginning to make everything new now.
> (Schillebeeckx *God the Future of Man*)

None of the books of the Bible, however, and certainly not the last book, the *Book of Revelation,* would see a straight-line development between work for the present good of this world and its final transformation. Coming through all of them is the realisation that the final victory of God's love will only be won through a seeming defeat and near despair: life through death as with Christ. The ultimate hope is through and beyond despair and the only ultimate sin is that which says "no" to that hope.

When he first began to make himself known to Israel, God spoke of himself as "I am who am". One way this can be translated is: "I am keeping my own counsel about who I am!" The tension will always be there for us between the God who keeps his own counsel about himself and God as he enters our world, our history, our flesh and blood. It is easy enough to opt for one or the other. The wholeness of Christianity, however, consists both of the strong faith that is a grasping in the dark of the wonder of God, and of making for God a home in our hearts:

> The Spirit and the Bride say, "Come". Let everyone who listens answer, "Come". Then let all who are thirsty come: all who want it may have the water of life, and have it free.
> (*Revelation 22:17*)

Suggested Scripture reading

The Acts of the Apostles; The Book of Revelation, chapters 1–3, 12, 21–22.